G4005038 20

The Spirit of Teaching

THE SPIRIT OF TEACHING

Edited by Julie Mars

Illustrated by Tatjana Krizmanic

ARIEL BOOKS

Andrews McMeel
Publishing

Kansas City

THE SPIRIT OF TEACHING

www.andrewsmcmeel.com

ISBN: 0-7407-0547-4
Library of Congress Catalog Card Number:
99-65541

CONTENTS

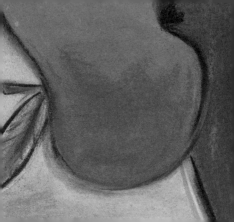

Introduction

Teacher. The word itself creates a rush of associations. Perhaps it brings fond memories of that special first-grade teacher who helped you unlock the mysteries of reading and writing. The music teacher who convinced you that you *were* good enough to audition for the school band. The algebra teacher who met with you after class until you could actually apply the principles of the Pythagorean theorem to questions on the SATs. The science teacher who helped you get a scholarship for college.

The simple word *teacher* seems to have emotion built into it, along with strong feel-

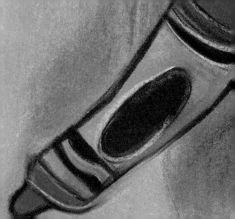

ings of respect, gratitude, and often, love. Teachers, more than any other adults except parents and family members, shape the ideas and values of our society's most precious resource — its children. They belong to the largest profession in the world (some thirty million strong) and it is no

The SPIRIT of TEACHING

exaggeration to say that their work directs, if not creates, the future.

Yet there are not many statues of teachers in public parks, not many stories passed down from generation to generation about important teachers, not many teachers among the list of heroes to whom our collective culture turns for inspiration. And whereas prestige for teachers is high all around the world, salaries typically are not.

So why do teachers do it? Why do they devote long and often unpaid hours to class planning, paper correcting, and impromptu student counseling? Cynics have said that there are only two good reasons to be a teacher: July and August. But the vast majority of teachers barely notice their summer vacation. They're too busy preparing to do an even better job the next year.

The truth is, great teachers have a mysterious and beautiful calling. They undertake the

job of inspiring children and providing the tools they need to master our complex world. Why? Because they believe that education liberates the individual. It explains the society we live in and helps create a better one. It is the foundation of freedom and the portal to a life full of challenge, community spirit, and, most important of all, meaning.

Teaching is more than an occupation. It's a way of life.

The SPIRIT of
TEACHING

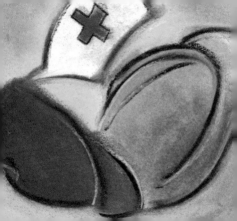

The Role of a Teacher

Teachers play multiple parts in students' lives. From kindergarten on up through the college years, a teacher can be at various times role model, parent, sponsor, peace officer, nurse, caretaker, challenger, referee, supporter, confessor, friend, and mentor. And the best teachers take each and every one of these roles seriously! Here are some former students' definitions of *teacher*:

The SPIRIT of

+
E
A
C
H
i
N
g

A teacher is someone who holds your future in his or her hands. Someone who always seemed "old" to me. Someone I had lots of respect for (although I'm not sure that's the case with many students and teachers these days). To me, a teacher was always someone who just plain knew more than I did—and probably still does!

—AMY, CINCINNATI, OH

The SPIRIT of +EACH-iNG

A teacher is a person who helps others to succeed.

—PAT, VERONA, PA

A teacher is . . . a helper.

—RENEE, TEMPLE, TX

A good teacher is a person who respects children and whose students, in turn, respect him or her. A person who knows how to make a child feel special. A person who is creative enough to open up whole worlds to young minds.

—SARAH, NORTHAMPTON, MA

Someone who challenges me to try harder, to think "outside of the box." A role model for learning. Some of the most difficult teachers I had are now, in retrospect, those I consider the best.

—SUE, TUCSON, AZ

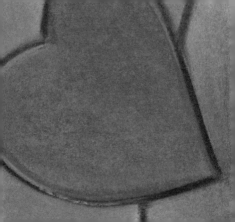

The Ten Qualities of Great Teachers

What makes a teacher exceptional? Does greatness derive from a set of skills that can be learned and developed or is unusual excellence in the classroom a God-given talent bestowed on a select few? Many of the greatest teachers are also the humblest. They understand the magic of learning, they respect and value their place in the process, and they thrive along with their students. But a closer look at classroom attitudes and methods of instruction reveals a commonality among the best of the best teachers.

The SPIRIT of TEACHING

Compassion

Understanding the challenges that all students face in the classroom, remembering the turbulence of learning the ways of the world, and being willing to reexperience the natural "growing pains" of school years are all part of the job for the gifted teacher. Feeling for—

and with—students is univer-sally acknowledged as funda-mental to success.

Creativity

Breathing life and excitement into the daily chores of school life calls for a bottomless well of creativity—and the best teachers seem to have access to one. Rarely fixed in their methods and typically willing to follow up on new inspirations rather than resist them, great teachers trust their creative instincts and search for alternative, more effective, and frequently, more entertaining ways to present lessons to students.

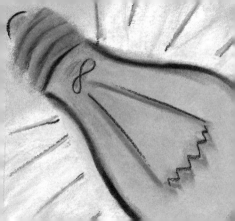

Dedication

A great teacher's dedication has two distinct parts. First, the teacher is devoted to students and determined to help them learn and grow. Second, he or she is strongly committed to professional development. Always up-to-date on the latest research and passionately involved in academic conversations with peers, dedicated teachers know that professionalism and achievement aren't limited by the four walls of the classroom.

Enthusiasm

Students need inspiration and enthusiastic teachers provide

it. Because they are happily engaged with their work, their passion and excitement is contagious . . . and their students reap enormous benefits. Enthusiasm stems from strong belief in the subject matter and in the importance of teaching it. Great teachers say enthusiasm builds on itself—exponentially.

Ethics

First, do no harm. These words, made famous in the Hippocratic oath in medical practice, apply to teachers as well. Teachers hold their students' self-esteem, confidence, and academic vulnerability in their hands. They can inspire but, unfortunately, they can also crush.

The SPIRIT of TEACHING

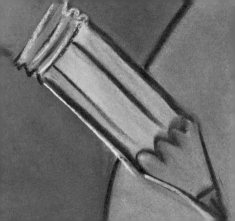

Great teachers remain acutely aware of ethical issues and difficulties in the classroom. They set (and model) high standards and help their students recognize and meet them.

Imagination

The mysterious power of the imagination allows a great

teacher to see each student's rich potential. Only then can teacher and student become cocreators of the student's new identity. This faith in a student's positive attributes and abilities permits teachers to challenge, push forward, and expect more. At the same time, it encourages students to pursue goals they might never have attempted.

Leadership

Ability to control and lead a classroom—preferably, with a soft touch—is the hallmark of an exceptional teacher. Some call it an ability to "work the group"; others say a great teacher sets an example for students to imitate. Successful leadership involves formulating a goal, assuming responsibility for reaching it, and inspiring students to do the same.

Listening

Many great teachers hold to the philosophy that teaching is

primarily listening and learning is primarily talking. They develop elaborate techniques to encourage students to express fearlessly their thoughts, observations, and questions. These teachers step back to give their students room to grow. They listen with extreme attention, carefully clarify misconceptions, and

The SPIRIT of

TEACHiNg

redirect energy, but mostly, they listen because they care.

Patience

Patience is a virtue great teachers must possess. The readiness to accept and work with students on their own level, even if it's frustrating at times, and the willingness to "try, try again"

when the first few attempts at instruction fail are essential to the art of teaching. Most of all, the teacher has to admit, accept, and honor the fact that the student, not the teacher, ultimately sets the pace.

Respect

An atmosphere of mutual, far-reaching respect between teacher and students is crucial in the classroom. Great teachers understand that respect is something they have to give in order to receive. Because they value the minds (and the personalities) they are helping to shape, treating students with courtesy, consideration, and regard is fundamental to their personal interaction—in and out of the classroom.

Teachers Who Touch Our Lives

Truly remarkable teachers don't come along every day. Every student who has ever been deeply affected by the dedication, wisdom, and inspiration of a particular teacher knows that the experience is rare and magical. Here are some stories from students who have known such teachers:

God bless Mr. McCann, a re-
tired navy captain and my
high school algebra teacher. I
had serious math anxiety and
thought, for some reason, that
I could not succeed at math. It
was so bad that I assumed
anything I thought was right
must be wrong. I will never
forget when he told me I was

The
SPIRIT
of

+
E
A
C
H
i
N
g

"nimble with my numbers" and that I should not waste time second-guessing myself on tests, because my first answers—the ones I crossed out—were generally right.

—RENEE, TEMPLE, TX

I went to a parochial school. My English and writing teacher seemed to always give me harsh grades no matter how hard I tried, although my other teachers gave me As and Bs readily.

He frustrated me . . . and he made me stretch. The most precious grade I ever received was the A I got on my final extemporaneous speech that semester. I'd love to find him and tell him that I'm a professional writer.

—PAT, VERONA, PA

My favorite teacher had a huge, red, cardboard dot. He was very funny and made us laugh a lot, but when he put that red cardboard dot on the blackboard, nobody said or breathed a word unless he said it was okay to do so.

This teacher also pushed us to the max. In his English class in eighth grade, I was writing three papers a week and our reading assignments included stories in magazines like *Atlantic Monthly* and *Harper's*.

He also commanded respect like few other people I know. He did this by working harder than any of us. No matter what, the day after we handed in our papers, we received them back with grades and extensive comments. (And he had loads of students, plus a family, etc.)

—SARAH, NORTHAMPTON, MA

I had teachers who were tough graders but at the same time gave us *lots* of feedback on papers and exams. We worked harder than we did in other

classes, but the rewards were greater.

At the end of the term, these same teachers often eased up a bit, basing each final grade on the student's individual effort and improvement. During the course, I resented the difficult exams and high standards, but after-

ward I was grateful that I had
been pushed.

—ALESIA, OAKLAND, CA

My English teacher once told
my mother that he thought I
could be president of the
United States one day. I've
never thought this was pos-
sible, but the confidence that

statement has given me is worth every word of it.

—SARAH, NORTHAMPTON, MA

When I was in first grade, I was pretty much the only one in my class who knew how to read. I think my original teacher suffered a heart attack that kept her from returning, so we had a long-term substitute.

The substitute was, in my eyes and my classmates' eyes, the best. We got to create books all the time. Lots of gluing and crayon drawings.

My mom wasn't real pleased about the piles of books I'd bring home, since the teacher just typed our captions on each

The
SPIRIT
of

T
E
A
C
H
I
N
G

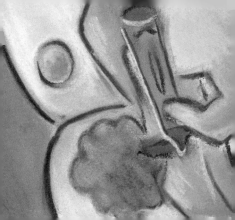

page for us. Reading, obviously, wasn't big in her curriculum. Except that we could read our very own books!

—AMY, CINCINNATI, OH

I particularly remember an elderly professor at Goddard College. During class, she'd offer around a plate of cookies,

The SPIRIT of TEACHING

or caviar, or whatever. If you said, "Yes," she'd give you one and if you said, "I don't know," she'd take that as a No, and even if you changed your mind right then it was too late.

My other teachers had taught me the value of not making up your mind too quickly. I don't remember this teacher's name, but she sure taught me the value of being decisive.

—MARY, FRONT ROYAL, VA

I think every teacher deserves the title of "remarkable."

—JOE, FAIRFIELD, CT

The SPIRIT of TEACHING

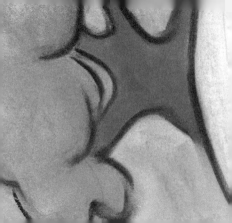

The Prime
of Mrs. Carol
Dervitz

Most of my teachers taught science or English or history, but my sixth-grade teacher, Carol Dervitz, was the rare teacher who taught about life. So much so that, more than three decades later, she and I are still great friends.

As students, we probably learned as much from Mrs.

Dervitz outside the classroom as we did in. If it was a beautiful day—and sometimes even if it wasn't—we would often be outdoors performing science experiments, creating art, taking class trips, and generally learning by doing as much as (if not more than) by studying. In fact, some of the text-

+
E
A
C
H
i
N
g

books we put into our desks in September were never seen again until the last day of school in June!

But who needed textbooks when we learned so much while having so much fun?

Some of us stayed in her classroom during lunchtime to rehearse the plays we had

written. And Mrs. Dervitz would stay right along with us. She said she preferred it to hanging out with the "whiners" in the teacher's lounge.

Often we would eat while we rehearsed and one day a student slipped on a banana peel during a scene. Mrs. Dervitz roared, "Keep that in! It's *funny!*"

We ended up performing our plays in front of the whole school. The shows were so successful that we also performed them in other schools and orphanages around our suburban New Jersey area. And of course, Mrs. Dervitz led the way as she drove us—sets, costumes, and all—in her car.

The SPIRIT of TEACHING

(The sixth-grade theater bug bit so strongly that I still write and direct plays professionally some thirty years later.)

As it turned out, the last day of our sixth-grade class was also the last day of Mrs. Dervitz's formal teaching career.

A group of us gladly gave up the first day of summer

vacation to go back to school and help her pack the decades of her teaching career into boxes. Mrs. Dervitz and her husband then moved to another town. He eventually became mayor there and, when he passed away, Mrs. Dervitz took over his office by popular acclaim.

In fact, popular acclaim follows her wherever she goes. With former students now living from California to Maine to Florida, Mrs. Dervitz is recognized *everywhere*. She still keeps in touch with many of her former pupils—including one from her student teaching days back in the 1930s.

"I'm so lucky!" she often says. "What other profession is there where you get to know so many wonderful people? And I learned more from them than they ever did from me."

And at the age of eighty-four, Carol Dervitz is still bringing her own brand of teaching to a new generation of students.

Her latest assignment is to go from school to school and talk to teenagers about controversial topics such as domestic violence, date rape, and abuse.

"When I walk into a classroom, I tell the students to call me 'Grandma,'" she explains. "Not everyone would remember my name, but they all remember Grandma. Then I tell them what an intelligent and wonderful group of students they are, because I don't think they hear enough of that these days.

"When I'm done with the lesson, I ask the students as they leave if they would touch me with a kind word or a hug.

Almost all of them do. And if I should go back to that school, when I'm walking down the hallway I hear them call out, 'Hi, Grandma!'

And so the prime of Mrs. Carol Dervitz continues as it has for more than half a century, for she continues to touch students with her kind words, hugs, and boundless enthusiasm.

And she thinks she's the lucky one . . .

—MITCHELL, FORT LAUDERDALE, FL

The SPIRIT of

+
E
A
C
H
i
N
9

Reading the signs

Astrologists believe that the stars and planets shape each individual's personality and destiny. But does this celestial typecasting extend to teaching style and classroom management? Does it forecast such qualities as intellectual excitement, creativity, and a dedication to communicating knowledge? For astrologers, the answer is a simple Yes. And for teachers? Call it an educated guess!

The
SPIRIT
of

TEACHiNg

ARIES

(March 21–April 20)

TEACHERS BORN UNDER the sign of the Ram are typically pioneering, rebellious, and enterprising. They forge new educational approaches and present even complex material in a dynamic, imaginative fashion. Students are drawn to the Aries warmth and spontaneity. No dull classrooms for Aries educators!

Wise Aries teachers will attempt to avoid the intellectual arrogance that comes naturally to them. Likewise, headstrong Aries teachers must learn to control and direct, rather than dominate, any difficult students and learning situations they might come across. But with their energy, enthusiasm, and sincerity, Aries teachers are typically treasured by both their peers and their students.

TAURUS

(April 21–May 21)

The SPIRIT of

♉ EARTH

PRACTICAL, GENTLE, AND patient, Taureans seem born to teach. They are thorough in their planning and dogged in their determination to make learning an interesting and pleasant challenge.

This sensible educational approach, along with their easygoing attitude toward life, transforms the occasional school-days drudgery into full-time fun.

Taurus teachers tend to be both opinionated and conservative—two characteristics they must face (and often suppress) in the classroom. They must also force themselves to experiment—not the path of choice for tradition-oriented Taurus. But Taurus teachers, determined to excel, find a variety of ways to combine the predictable with the magical in their daily classroom performance.

T
E
A
C
H
I
N
G

GEMINI

(May 22–June 21)

GEMINI TEACHERS TEND to live in their minds—exactly the right place for inspiration! They are versatile, witty, and lively and can easily transform the classroom into a combination think tank and

The SPIRIT of

† EACHINg

playground. Students respond to Gemini's high-spirited brilliance, while Gemini teachers genuinely appreciate the passions of youth—and are determined to help shape them.

One major challenge is organization. Because Geminis dread routine tasks, their style is often scattered and chaotic. Fortunately, youthful minds can cope quite easily with such teacherly turmoil. But perhaps Geminis should ask themselves, wouldn't it be more productive if they actually *knew* where their grade books were at any given moment?

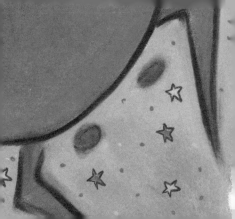

CANCER

(June 22–July 23)

CANCER IS RULED BY THE Moon—and the Moon gives Cancerian teachers a wealth of classroom talents. They are typically artistic, imaginative, wise, and unpredictable. And because Cancerian teachers are super-

The SPIRIT of

✝
E
A
C
H
I
N
G

sensitive to their students, they frequently discover alternative educational paths to each individual—and manage to keep the whole group involved in learning too.

However, Cancerian teachers run the risk of too much involvement. They must remember to

set boundaries for themselves—
and to guard them. All work and
no play is exhausting and it's up
to each Cancerian teacher to
sidestep this predictable pitfall.

The
SPIRIT
of

+
C
A
N
C
E
R

LEO

(July 24–August 23)

ALL TEACHERS KNOW THAT the classroom is a stage . . . and there's no more willing performer than a Leo. In fact, Leos crave the spotlight and are happiest when it's a solo act. The good news is that they also deliver. For Leo teachers, it's not about dramatic antics; it's about the real thing: education. Their theatricality is just an added bonus!

Leo teachers love a challenge, and their creativity is boundless. Add to that their sunny dispositions and natural authority, and it's a recipe for school success. Once Leos learn to curb their impatience, they find smooth sailing in the classroom—and in life.

The SPIRIT of

+
E
A
C
H
I
N
G

VIRGO

(August 24–September 23)

SHARP ANALYTICAL SKILLS, an inquiring mind, and mental precision—these are the qualities of typical Virgo teachers. Their practicality compels them to streamline their teaching techniques into

The
SPIRIT
of

✝
E
A
C
H
I
N
G

models of efficiency and their humanitarian impulses guarantee that the ends are both respectful and interesting.

Virgos have the astrological reputation of being hypercritical. Careful Virgo teachers channel these powers of observation and analysis into positive feedback—and students thrive. Virgo teachers take a mental spark and fan it until it blazes with intellectual brilliance; then they step aside and let their students shine.

LIBRA

(September 24–October 23)

A IR SIGNS TEND TO BE analytical, objective, and intellectually oriented. Libra is an air sign and Libran teachers personify these airy traits. They value balance, careful examination of all sides of an

The SPIRIT of ♎ Libra

issue, and fairness above all. Consequently, they are gifted, thoughtful teachers.

The Libran teacher seeks (and builds) a harmonious classroom in which each opinion is valued and each student learns to apply rules of logic—and humanitarianism. Librans

are a mysterious mix of ideal-
istic and realistic, a combination that allows them to
respect and accept the students as they are and simultaneously to prepare them to be
all that they can be.

The
SPIRIT
of
T
E
A
C
H
I
N
g

SCORPIO

(October 24–November 22)

SCORPIO TEACHERS ARE like private detectives: They won't rest until they have the right answer. Creative as well, they typically transform learning into an intriguing puzzle. Their students are hap-

The SPIRIT of TEACHiNg

pily drawn into the game by the Scorpio magnetism and humor.

Teachers born under this sign tend to be intuitive in their approach. They rely on textbooks to a certain extent; after that, it's a mystery! Scorpio teachers combine intense powers of observation with clarity

in explanation. They also in-
stinctively know the best way
to encourage students to take
risks—and reap the educational
rewards forever after.

The
SPIRIT
of
T
E
A
C
H
i
n
g

SAGITTARIUS

(November 23–December 21)

FOR SAGITTARIUS TEACHERS, logic is everything. They are on a quest for answers and, once they find them, they feel compelled to spread the news. Because Sagittarians are typically charming, witty, and

The
SPIRIT
of

† T
E E
A A
C C
H H
i i
N N
g g

bright, their messages are quickly embraced and students learn without struggle.

Sagittarians are often travelers—in the real world and the inner realm of the imagination too. Consequently, they bring vitality, freshness, and a broad perspective to teaching.

Interested in the well-being of the planet and every being on it, Sagittarian teachers cover the basics and simultaneously instill an awareness of the big picture in one brilliant stroke.

The SPIRIT of

CAPRICORN

CAPRICORN

(December 22–January 20)

THE ASTROLOGICAL SIGN Capricorn is ruled by the planet Saturn, which symbolizes the forces of constriction, limitation, and self-discipline. This often leads to a very serious, practical approach to both

The SPIRIT of EARTH ♑

teaching and classroom management. Capricorn teachers typically rely on the tried-and-true . . . and they get results.

Common sense and a gift for planning also characterize the Capricornian. This teacher is not one to "wing it" or show up in the classroom under-prepared. The typical learning atmosphere is one of quiet industry and goal orienta-tion—a winning situation for the teacher as well as the stu-dents, who thrive under Capricorn's careful, professional direction.

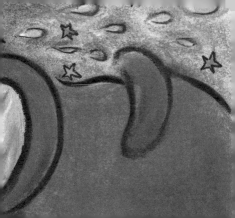

AQUARIUS

(January 21–February 19)

BORN IN AN AIR SIGN, Aquarians make excellent teachers because they love the life of the mind. Ideas, concepts, and theories are food to Aquarians and putting their ideas into practice is a reward

The SPIRIT of

+
E
A
C
H
i
N
g

in itself. They love a challenge and often consider teaching the greatest challenge of them all.

Aquarian teachers tend to be creative, confident, and cooperative. They believe that learning is a group effort—and the bigger the group, the better the effort. So it's unlikely that an Aquarius will elect to teach by the lecture method. Instead, learning becomes an educational scavenger hunt— and everybody, including the teacher, wins!

The SPIRIT of TEACHiNg

PISCES

(February 20–March 20)

INTUITIVE, COMPASSIONATE, and wise, Pisces teachers take a gentle approach to teaching. They are able to encourage students without pressuring them and they create a safe, comfortable class-

The SPIRIT of TEACHING

room atmosphere in which even the most shy students can learn to shine.

A rare combination of managerial skill and dreamy imagination, Pisces teachers slip across educational borders that stymie other professionals. They are innovators with-

out bothersome egos and they
are not prone to rest on their
laurels. There's always another
task to complete, another idea
to teach, and another student
in need of inspiration.

Learned Advice

Advice is a funny thing. Often, when we're young, we don't appreciate all of the wisdom available to us. "I know all that; you don't have to tell me" might be a familiar refrain. But lucky for us, great teachers don't give up on us—they never stop trying to guide and prepare us for the world ahead. And the lessons that stay with us often have less to do with fractions and battle-fields than with how best to make our way through life.

My best teacher told me to work my abilities, not to let them lie fallow.

—PAT, VERONA, PA

In college I had a very unconventional English professor. He told us one day that he didn't like to read. He also said that he gained most of his inspiration and satisfaction in life from reading. He didn't seem worried that this might sound contradictory—he was more interested in waking us up, in telling us two contradictory but true things, even if they puzzled us.

One spring day as he was lecturing with the classroom windows open, a jet went right over campus, drowning out several of his sentences. He didn't stop talking. Later, several students asked him to

The SPIRIT of

T
E
A
C
H
i
n
g

repeat what they had missed. His response was, "You're going to miss some things in real life. Don't worry about what's gone; pay attention to what you have."

—SUE, TUCSON, AZ

The best advice given to me by a teacher was made in a gesture. My history professor in college realized that I just wasn't "getting his point" in class, since my exam responses left something to be desired.

He offered me extra help— he basically taught me to take notes, and after his lectures met with me to review the material. His help to me was a

The SPIRIT of

TEACHiNG

wonderful statement. Even though I was in a college of over twenty thousand students, he taught me not only how to "pay attention" and take good notes quickly but also that I wasn't just a number or blank face in his class.

I made sure to take his classes throughout my four

years of college, and we are still in touch today. I consider myself lucky to have met someone who truly enjoyed his profession and shared his knowledge with me.

—AMY, CINCINNATI, OH

My high school English teacher taught all levels of classes, from remedial to advanced. He used to say that the remedial classes were more lively and imaginative than the honors classes, where the students often seemed conventional and conservative in their thinking.

The SPIRIT of THINKING

One of his methods for inspiring his students to read was to let them choose one book from their own area of interest (such as a basketball player's life story or a history of race cars) and write a book report on it. "It almost doesn't matter *what* you read, as long as you read," he used to say.

"If you know how to read, you can teach yourself. If you can't, you're out of luck."

—STORM, KINGMAN, AZ

My favorite teacher told me that if I wanted to be a writer, I had to write every day—every single day. And he's right.

—SARAH, NORTHAMPTON, MA

Movers, Shakers, and Great Innovators

Socrates (c. 470–399 B.C.)

Socrates, the ancient Greek philosopher and educator, is often better known for his death than for his life. In 399 B.C., he was found guilty of "corrupting the youth" of Athens and sentenced to die. Refusing a chance for amnesty through exile, Socrates willingly drank poison hemlock and perished, surrounded by his grief-stricken students—a scene which has been depicted in many famous works of art.

But what aspect of his teaching style so threatened his society that he had to die for it? Or perhaps a more important question is this: Why has his

The SPIRIT of

THINKING

method of teaching continued to thrive for over two millennia?

To answer these questions, it is important to understand that Socrates was more than a man; he was a symbol of the changing values of his society. Before Socrates' time, teaching was done primarily in the home by family members. Because of this continuity, few new ideas were introduced and skepticism was discouraged.

Socrates smashed that model and at the same time turned teaching into a well-respected profession. He is personally responsible for shifting the locus of education from the home to the institution. In fact,

The SPIRIT of

+
E
A
C
H
I
N
g

the prototype university was started by Socrates' famous student, Plato.

Socrates was also the first teacher to emphasize the importance of ideas, logic, and abstract thought. He restructured learning into a question-and-answer dialogue between students and teachers. This new dialogue system had three effects: It led to deep investigation into the "why" of things; it stripped family members of their former status and authority as teachers; and it encouraged students to question the status quo, including the social structure. Thus, Socrates was viewed by the elders as a dangerous influence—and by the youth as a hero and role model.

Believed to be the first teacher to promote the importance of rational thought and the written (as opposed to the merely spoken) word, Socrates is still revered as the forefather of education as we know and accept it today.

Thomas Jefferson (1743-1826)

Out of his numerous life-time achievements, Thomas Jefferson listed only three in his self-composed epitaph: author of the Declaration of Independence, author of the Statute of Virginia, and "Father of the University of Virginia." Clearly he considered his part in creating an American university system equal in importance to his role in founding the country—and more worthy of mention than his two terms as the country's third president!

But Thomas Jefferson's impact on American education neither began nor ended with the University of Virginia. During most of his adult life, he championed basic education for every person, regardless of wealth or family status.

Jefferson's long-range objectives for his home state (and later, for the country) included four distinct elements: free elementary schools for every citizen; a merit scholarship system under which poor students could attend secondary school; a public university in which qualified, economically deprived students repaid their education through service to the state; and a private "true" university.

Jefferson proposed his first

bill for educational reform in 1779—just three years after the end of the American Revolution—and he continued his crusade for universal education until his death.

Americans have Thomas Jefferson—a political radical and an educational innovator—to thank for the educa-

The SPIRIT of

+
E
A
C
H
·
N
9
z
i
N

tional system we take so much for granted.

Anne Sullivan (1866-1936)

The whole world knows Helen Keller—the deaf, mute, and blind child who overcame her handicaps to blaze a trail of remarkable accomplishments: a Radcliffe degree, several works of nonfiction (at least two of which have become modern-day classics), and the foundation of the American Foundation for the Blind and other agencies dedicated to assisting the handicapped.

But Helen Keller, as she herself often commented, would never have become the inspir-

The SPIRIT of

T
E
A
C
H
I
N
g

173

ing, independent figure she was without the perseverance, creativity, and loyalty of her beloved teacher, Anne Sullivan.

Born in Massachusetts in 1866, Anne Sullivan suffered a childhood illness, which seriously weakened her eyesight. At age ten, she became a student at the state infirmary for the blind in Tewksbury. She later transferred to the Perkins Institute for the Blind in Boston, where she learned the touch (or manual) alphabet and the Braille system.

Her eyesight was partially restored through a series of operations shortly after her graduation. It was only a year

The
SPiRiT
of

T
E
A
C
H
i
N
g

later that she undertook the monumental challenge of teaching Helen Keller, an angry, unruly seven-year-old, to understand and use the manual alphabet and eventually to read, write, and even speak.

After a month of intense frustration with her young student, Anne Sullivan made

an enormous breakthrough. At the family's water pump, she managed to show Helen that the water gushing forth was related to the hand signs Sullivan made for it. Once Helen realized that "everything had a name," her world suddenly opened up— and Anne Sullivan was there to guide her through it.

Accompanying Helen to her classes at the Perkins Institute, the Cambridge School for Young Ladies, and finally Radcliffe College, Anne Sullivan used the manual alphabet to instantly communicate the course content to her lifelong pupil. Keller graduated with honors from Radcliffe in 1904 but was saddened that the college refused to acknowledge Anne Sullivan's efforts, without which Keller could not have succeeded.

In 1905, Anne Sullivan married Harvard instructor and literary critic John Macy but the marriage was short-lived. Sullivan remained by Helen Keller's side, collaborating

with her on writing, fund-
raising, and lecture projects,
for almost fifty years. She died
in 1936. Helen Keller immortal-
ized her great teacher, com-
panion, and friend in a tribute
published in 1955.

The
SPIRIT
of
TEACHING

Booker T. Washington (1856-1915)

Booker Taliaferro Washington was born into slavery in 1856. His early life, fraught with hardship, included hard labor in a coal mine—before the age of ten.

He had a rudimentary education and a big dream: to improve the lot of black people in the United States. And before Booker T. Washington died at the age of fifty, he had indeed become a leading spokesperson for African-Americans and had created one of the most powerful educational institutions of its time.

Washington's path toward greatness began in earnest at

sixteen when he accepted a jan-
itorial position at the Hampton
Normal and Agricultural Institute in Virginia in exchange
for room, board, and tuition. He
completed his studies, particularly excelling in rhetoric and
public speaking, and soon
joined the faculty of the
Hampton Institute.

The
SPIRIT
of

THANKSGIVING

In 1881, his life changed. Washington moved to Tuskegee, Alabama, to establish a school recently approved by the state government. The fact that no money had been allotted for building the school did not discourage him. He borrowed funds from the Hampton Institute, invested in a kiln, and manufactured bricks for the building. Together with his four hundred black students, Booker T. Washington constructed the Tuskegee Institute. Despite its shaky start, the school quickly began to thrive.

The institute taught vocational as well as academic subjects; students were encouraged

TEACHING

to focus on thriftiness, hard work, and constant self-improvement. Washington's educational efforts soon earned him much notoriety and his fund-raising intensified. Millionaire philanthropists such as Andrew Carnegie and John Wanamaker became patrons of the Tuskegee Institute, but the policy-making decisions remained in Washington's hands.

Booker T. Washington's popular autobiography, *Up from Slavery*, was translated into a dozen languages. He became a trusted adviser to Presidents Theodore Roosevelt and William Taft and bankrolled a voting-rights legal case all the way to

The SPIRIT of TEACHING

the Supreme Court. But his heart remained at the Tuskegee Institute and, after a lifetime of achievement that guaranteed his place in history, he died there on November 14, 1915.

John Dewey (1859–1952)

Born on a small farm in rural Vermont and trained as a

grammar school teacher, John Dewey was perhaps an unlikely candidate for the honor of becoming, by many accounts, the single most important American thinker of his era. But that is exactly what happened.

A teacher first and later a philosopher, Dewey stepped forward to revitalize the worn-

The SPIRIT of TEACHING

out educational system in the United States. Heavily influenced by both Darwinism and the newly emerging science of psychology, Dewey encouraged teachers and students to question their habitual approaches to problem solving. He insisted that the goal of all

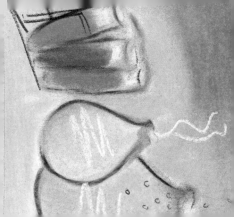

philosophy (and especially the philosophy of education) is to solve human problems and that, therefore, success in learning required active engagement with the subject at hand. In order to be meaningful, he said, philosophy had to be applied to the real world—and it had to work.

Dewey encouraged teachers to abandon the traditional method of memorize-and-repeat instruction and instead replace it with a system in which students learned how—and why—to think for themselves. Among his most valuable (and at the time, radical) innovations are: the emphasis

THE SPIRIT OF

TEACHING

on actual experience or, as Dewey called it, "learning by doing"; the need for a student-centered classroom rather than an authoritarian one; and the use of in-class, group activities to foster creativity, cooperation, and a hands-on approach to problem solving.

In addition to his progressive educational reforms, Dewey served as president of the American Philosophical Association and the American Association of University Professors. He also helped found both the Teachers Union and the American Civil Liberties Union and published more than twenty-five books on the philosophy of teaching.

The SPIRIT of

TEACHING

Mary McLeod Bethune
(1875–1955)

Mary McLeod Bethune, African-American educator, was born in Mayesville, South Carolina, the fifteenth child of Patsy and Samuel McLeod. The first of her family to be born free, Mary McLeod soon committed herself to an unlikely goal, given the poverty of her family: She wanted an education.

Her determination to learn to read attracted the attention of a church teacher, Miss Emma J. Wilson, who tutored Mary for several years. At age twelve, Mary won an extremely competitive scholarship sponsored by Mary Crossman, a seamstress

The SPIRIT of TEACHINg

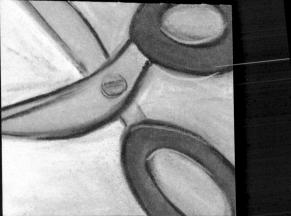

who wanted to use her life savings to educate one black child.

Expecting to become a missionary, Mary McLeod attended the Moody Bible Institute, but it was not her destiny. Instead, she accepted temporary teaching positions in Georgia and South Carolina. She met and married Albertus Bethune in

TEACHING

1898. A few years later, she had three significant dreams that she believed instructed her to move south and start a school for African-American children.

She arrived in Daytona, Florida, in 1903 with one dollar and fifty cents to her name. Only a year later, through tireless fund-raising, she opened

her school. By 1905, it had
expanded to one hundred
girls; the following year, it
expanded again. When one of
her students was refused treat-
ment at a whites-only clinic,
Mary McLeod Bethune founded
a hospital; shortly afterward,

The
SPIRIT
of

+
E
A
C
H
I
N
G

she began a farm, where students learned self-sufficiency along with botany.

Mary McLeod Bethune's crusade to educate African-American girls culminated in the establishment of the Bethune-Crokman College in 1925. She became a respected spokesperson for the National

Association of Colored People, the Red Cross, and the Council of Negro Women. Additionally, she was a valued adviser to Presidents Harry S. Truman and Franklin Delano Roosevelt.

When Mary McLeod Bethune died in 1955, more than three thousand people attended her funeral. Written on her tomb-

The SPIRIT of

TEACHING

stone is this simple, eloquent message: "She has given her best that others may lead a more abundant life."

Hannah Breece (1859–1940)

According to her niece, Jane Jacobs, who edited her autobiography *A Schoolteacher in Old Alaska*, Hannah Elizabeth

Breece had a thoroughly unremarkable upbringing and early adulthood.

Born in a small town in rural Pennsylvania, she grew up on a farm with her parents and eleven siblings, attended the Bloomsburg Academy for teacher training, and at twenty, launched a respectable career in the Bloomsburg elementary schools. Choosing to remain single, Hannah Breece slowly ascended the academic ladder, ultimately becoming the principal of an elementary school.

But somewhere in her heart, she must have yearned for adventure. This spirit led her, at the close of the nineteenth century, to accept an unlikely appointment from the United States Department of the Interior. Traveling by covered wagon, she spent four years on the Navajo, Ute, Hopi, and Sioux reservations in the Southwest. Her mission: to inform the Native Americans about educational options available to them.

In an even more surprising move, at the age of forty-five, Breece agreed to go alone to the wilds of Alaska—for the sum of six hundred dollars a year—to teach Eskimos, Aleuts, Athabascans, and Kenai people to read, write, and hold their own in the modern world that was pressing ever closer to them.

Hannah Breece's arrival in Alaska marked the beginning of a fourteen-year sojourn during which she faced (and beat) seemingly insurmountable odds. Says Jane Jacobs, "She camped out with Indians! She held a hundred wild dogs at bay by herself and escaped them! . . . A bear almost ate

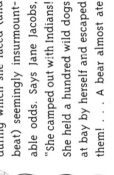

her right from her bed!"

Why, in the early years of the twentieth century, would she have chosen a life of such challenge and discomfort? Because Hannah Breece "had utter faith that American civilization held the keys to overcoming ignorance, poverty, disease, and superstition."

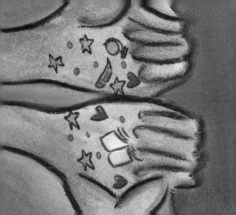

Isolated and alone in the Alaskan wilderness, committed to preparing native children for the rigors of an increasingly mechanized world, and determined to create the schools she had been hired to establish, she doggedly pursued her goals, recording her trials and triumphs in letters and diaries.

The SPIRIT of

TEACHING

At age fifty-nine, her mission complete, she left Alaska and settled in McMinnville, Oregon, where she taught for several more years before retirement. Hannah Breece died at eighty, perhaps the last of the frontier teachers.

Christa McAuliffe (1948-1986)

Sharon Christa McAuliffe has been described by many as the all-American girl-next-door. Her parents, Grace and Ed Corrigan, lived in low-income housing until Ed finished college, landed a good accounting job, and moved the family into their own house in the

Boston suburbs. Family life was stable and happy.

Christa grew up to marry her high school sweetheart and have two children. As a young wife, she helped put her husband through law school, and as a dedicated teacher, she ultimately earned a distinctive honor: She was selected to be the first private citizen to journey in space aboard the space shuttle *Challenger*. Sadly, the whole world witnessed the tragedy of the explosion that took Christa McAuliffe's life on January 28, 1986.

Those who knew her say that she would like to be remembered for her optimism, classroom creativity, and dedication to the art of teaching. As a social studies teacher, Christa McAuliffe took her students on field trips to gritty, real-life courtrooms, required her economics students to learn about the stock market from professional stockbrokers, and orchestrated controversial mock trials in her class on law. She sparkled in and out of the classroom. "I touch the future," she frequently said. "I teach."

Christa McAuliffe constantly sought new ways to expand her personal horizons. She was determined to live each moment to the fullest—

The SPIRIT of + C H i N g

and she encouraged her students to do the same. When she entered NASA's competition for a place in space, one of 11,500 applicants, she hardly dared hope to win, although space travel had been a secret wish of hers since adolescence. But she was chosen, and the rest is history.

Christa McAuliffe left behind a beloved husband, two children, and hundreds of students who will never forget her.

Jaime Escalante (b. 1930)

A native of Bolivia, Jaime Escalante, like many immigrants, came to America in search of a better life for himself and his children. He found one. But his is not a typical rags-to-riches tale. Escalante did not end up in a mansion overlooking the sea; he lived and worked in the barrio of East Los Angeles. He did not drive a Mercedes Benz or a Cadillac; he

THE SPIRIT OF
+
E
A
C
H
i
N
g

drove an ancient Volkswagen Beetle. He did not make money; he made miracles.

When Jaime Escalante arrived in the United States, he left behind a firmly established teaching career. He had been a physics teacher at San Calixto School in La Paz for many years. But his expertise meant little in his new country and he soon discovered he would be unable to teach unless he repeated his education at an American college.

Taking a job as a restaurant janitor to support his family, he began his studies. As he worked his way through college, he became the restaurant's head

The SPIRIT of

THANKS GIVING

chef. After graduating, he found a job at Garfield High, an East Los Angeles school beset with the predictable problems of an inner-city school: gang violence, poor facilities, burned-out teachers, a high dropout rate, and a distinct lack of hope.

The
SPIRIT
of
TEACHING

In fact, Garfield High was in danger of losing its accreditation. Ninety-five percent of the student body was Hispanic; the majority were poverty stricken; many came from families in which no one spoke English or had ever completed high school—or even elementary school.

Yet these same underprivi-leged students—under Jaime Escalante's inspired mix of tough love, high expectations, and deep caring—soon broke all academic records by pass-ing the extremely difficult Advanced Placement exam in calculus . . . with flying colors.

Because Escalante believed

The SPIRIT of

TEACHING

in his students, they believed in themselves. And when the results of the test were questioned by suspicious officials ("How could a poor school like Garfield produce so many mathematics wizards?"), Escalante exposed the underlying academic racism that often

$$a^2 + b^2 = c^2$$

$$2 + 2 = 4$$

$$x^2 \div y^2$$

cripples the chances of inner-city students.

Escalante's triumph was brought to public attention through the movie *Stand and Deliver*. He has been called the best teacher in America. But Jaime Escalante's formula for academic success is simple: Believe in students, push them to believe in themselves, and never fall victim to "I can't" or "They can't" attitudes.

Howard Gardner (b. 1943)

There's a revolution afoot in American education and its commander-in-chief is, by many accounts, Harvard psychologist and neurologist,

The SPIRIT of

† E A C H i N g

Howard Earl Gardner. A modern-day David, Gardner is attempting to slay a long-established educational Goliath: intelligence assessment.

As codirector of Project Zero at the Harvard Graduate School of Education, Gardner is determined not only to reinterpret how people learn but also to revise long-held (and to Gardner, arbitrary and out-moded) standards for the measurement of intelligence. He questions the traditional focus on math and verbal skills as the primary means of evaluation, and argues that

The SPIRIT of

+
E
A
C
H
I
N
g

intelligence has a much wider scope than many educators believe.

If a child is reflective and introspective, says Gardner, then that is an indication of a specific kind of intelligence. If he is good at movement or dance or if she has a talent for laying out mock villages on the kindergarten floor, those are intelligences too.

To date, Gardner has named eight distinct intelligences—six of which have nothing to do with math or verbal skill. Rather, they focus on such hitherto undervalued skill areas as music, spatial relations, human relations,

and the ability to categorize information or use one's body.

Gardner challenges teachers to recognize and nurture *each* form of intelligence. The natural results of this system—a system that values alternative assessment—are many: increased student self-esteem,

The
SPIRIT
of

more respect for diversity, and a chance for each student to excel and teach others.

Howard Gardner is a man driven to change the educational world. And he *is* changing it: every time one more teacher learns to approach intelligence as plural and not singular in nature and every time one more student takes pride in his or her gifts and learns to respect and value those of others.

The
SPIRIT
of
+
E
A
C
H
i
n
g

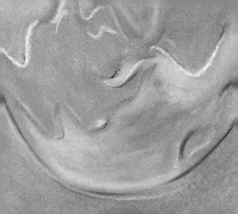

Teaching
around
the World

JAPAN

Though traditional Japanese society has undergone rapid changes due to the influence of Western culture, many ancient ways continue. One is the *kyoiku mama,* or "education mama." All schooling for college-bound youth inevitably ends in the highly competitive, university entrance exams, so it is typically the mother's duty and responsibility to encourage, prod, and at times, force her children to stay education-ally on track.

And it's not only the high school students who face stiff competition: Even three-year-old children take entrance exams for the best preschools. Thus, in the traditional Japanese family, the mother is the first and often foremost teacher.

Within the elementary and high school system, teachers are typically shown great respect. Students often avoid eye contact with their teacher as an acknowledgment of the teacher's superior status and classrooms are silent—except for the sound of the teacher's voice.

For college-bound students, though, the school day doesn't end with the final bell. More than half of all high school students (and about 40 percent of fourth- through sixth-graders) attend intensive "cram schools" that add up to five hours per day to the student's academic workload.

LATIN AMERICA

Because of the wide economic spectrum in Central

and South America, general-
izations about education—and
about teachers—are difficult to
make, but it is safe to say that
secondary and university education are available to only a
very small percentage of the
population.

Most Latin American coun-
tries require three to six years

The
SPIRIT
of
TEACHING

of elementary school, but in rural areas, potential students are often unable to attend at all. High schools (called middle schools in Latin America) generally charge tuition, which limits enrollment. And even in the most industrialized countries, the percentage of stu-

dents able to pursue a college education ranges from 1 to 7.

Given these factors, it is no surprise that most Latin American countries suffer from a severe shortage of trained teachers. Elementary school teachers typically have the equivalent of a high school education, although, in many isolated areas, these teachers have completed no more than elementary school themselves. And while some secondary school teachers have a university education, elementary school teachers are commonly promoted to teach alongside them because of the shortage of properly trained teaching professionals.

Salaries are low, and the majority of teachers must take on second jobs to make ends meet. But respect for learning—and teachers—is high. The work itself and the satisfaction of being addressed respectfully as "Teacher" bring their own rewards to the dedicated teachers of Central and South America.

INDIA

In multilingual, multicultural India, providing basic education is a daunting daily challenge faced by nearly four million teachers. But this commitment to learning—and particularly, literacy—is fairly recent. In historical terms, about fifty years. Today, in a country of eight hundred million people, more than half the adult population is illiterate.

The teachers of India are using their limited resources to help ensure that this grim statistic does not carry over to future generations.

Education in India is both free and mandatory until age fourteen. About 85 percent of children attend grades one

through five, and classes are typically conducted in the dialect of the region.

In grades six through ten, however, the percentage of students attending drops to about 35. Reasons for this are complex. Many children quit school because they must secure jobs to help support the family; others drop out because many of the secondary schools (and almost all the institutions of higher learning) conduct their classes exclusively in English. Only about 6 percent of students attend college or university.

The government of India has made education a priority and committed funds to building schools, training teachers, and purchasing books and other educational materials. But demand still far outweighs supply. Despite such formidable odds, however, India's teachers rise to the occasion each day, bringing literacy skills to both urban and rural areas and helping India and its people meet the challenges of the next millennium.

KENYA

Most of the formal education in Africa, and certainly in Kenya, was pioneered in eighteenth- and early

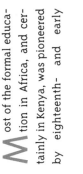

nineteenth-century Protestant and Roman Catholic missionaries, who viewed literacy as a necessary tool for Bible instruction. Opportunities for education were extremely limited during this time and hinged upon acceptance of Christian doctrine.

The SPIRIT of TEACHING

The school system grew during the colonial period, which spanned the latter half of the nineteenth and first half of the twentieth century, though classrooms were typically racially segregated. Kenyan education took a huge step forward after independence was declared in 1963, when the

government attempted to respond to the popular demand
for more and better schools.

Kenya still has no system of
mandatory schooling. However,
modern Kenyans tend to see
education as the primary means
for social advancement and
they send their children to
school. Over three-quarters of

THE
SPIRIT
OF

+
E
A
C
H
I
N
g
2
✎

Kenyan children attend free public elementary schools. Unfortunately, at the high school level where students must pay tuition fees, the attendance rate drops drastically to just over 13 percent. The government helps finance about half the schools in the

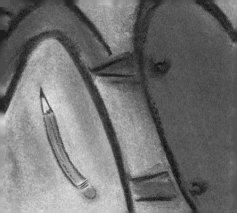

country; the rest, called *haram-bee* (the Swahili word for "pulling together"), or self-help schools, are privately run.

While there are many technical training institutes in Kenya, there are only three national universities. As in other underdeveloped countries, teachers are in great demand. While the working conditions and the remunera- tion are often less than desir- able, these teachers forge courageously ahead, improv- ing their country and the lives of their people.

The SPIRIT of TEACHING

THIS BOOK WAS DESIGNED
AND TYPESET IN TRIPLEX BY
ANN OBRINGER OF BEDFORD, NY.